COME
AWAY

Myra Cohn Livingston
COME AWAY

PICTURES BY
Irene Haas

A MARGARET K. MC ELDERRY BOOK

Atheneum · New York
AN ALADDIN BOOK

To Aga / M.C.L.
To Alfreda / I.H.

Published by Atheneum
All rights reserved
Text copyright © 1974 by Myra Cohn Livingston
Illustrations copyright © 1974 by Irene Haas
Published simultaneously in Canada by Collier Macmillan Canada, Inc.
Manufactured by Pearl-Pressman-Liberty Printers
Philadelphia, Pennsylvania
ISBN 0-689-71046-1
First Aladdin Edition

Come away, O human child!
To the waters and the wild
With a faery, hand in hand,
For the world's more full of weeping than you
   can understand.

From "The Stolen Child"
by William Butler Yeats

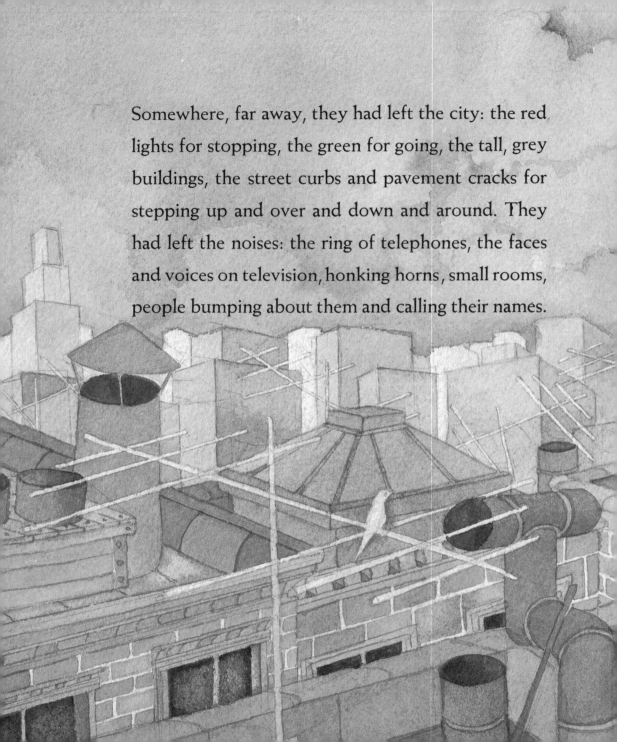

Somewhere, far away, they had left the city: the red lights for stopping, the green for going, the tall, grey buildings, the street curbs and pavement cracks for stepping up and over and down and around. They had left the noises: the ring of telephones, the faces and voices on television, honking horns, small rooms, people bumping about them and calling their names.

They had left all this behind, one late afternoon, and had come to a place where trees grew tall over their heads, where leaves rustled under their feet, where a path paved with earth told them to take off their shoes.

"It smells of green," Mark said.

"It smells new," Alice answered.

They walked off the path into the waist-high grass and came to a spot where a patch of wild flowers grew.

Alice picked one and put it in her hat.

"Look at me," she told Mark.

But Mark had stooped down, too, and was picking another flower with a long stem, which he stuck into his hat.

"Look at me," he said.

Then they heard a gushing sound and ran past the flowers to a low stone wall that bordered a stream. Alice climbed over the wall to where huge rocks lay. She picked up a piece of tree bark and threw it into the water, watching the eddies of the stream swallow it up. Mark had climbed up on the wall. He had found something.

"Whatever she is," he mumbled, "she's black and round like a tire without any center, and has two antennae trying to poke off my hat.

"Whoever she is," he muttered again, shifting ahead on his knees, "she's making her own sticky white roadway all over the wall."

But Alice wasn't listening. Far off, maybe nine million miles away, she had caught sight of something silhouetted against the sun. It was so tiny she had to

squint hard and try to keep her balance, her toes curled tightly against the rocks where she stood. "Imagine," she thought, "imagine a thing so near the sun—it will take him a long time to get down to earth."

"Come look," Mark urged Alice. "Turn around and ask her who she is. She won't answer me."

"Sssshhh—I'm calling to him to come back," she answered. "The sun is going down quickly and he'll be late for supper."

Mark inched forward. The stones that made up the wall were smooth and cold. His starry coat kept him warm, but the soles of his feet were growing chilly. He could see the stream gurgling below him, sparkling with glints of light from the last rays of the sun, but it was growing late and the woods would soon be dark.

"Are you listening?" he asked Alice again. "I hear the sun going down."

"Help me to call to him," she answered. "Tell him

that the stars have found their way into the sky and the moon is thin and hungry."

"I can't," said Mark, poking his face up closer to the hard blackness. "I must find out who she is before we have to go."

The flowers were closing their petals now, folding them carefully together, and the two that Mark and Alice had picked were beginning to droop into their faces. The water was changing from blue to gray. A breeze made them both shiver, and from somewhere a voice called their names.

"Don't listen," Mark cried, shoving his hat further down over his head.

"I won't," Alice answered, tossing her head and sticking her fingers into her ears.

The sun was turning red now, striping the sky with pinks and oranges. Alice curled her toes tightly around the rocks and made her hands into a hollow around her mouth. "Come back," she called, "come back."

"He won't answer you," Mark told her. "Nothing wants to answer us."

"I know he will," Alice said. "If I wait he will answer."

"Then I'll wait for her to answer too," Mark said.

Both children were silent. Insects hummed down from the tall trees; the water bubbled below. Suddenly a strange sound, not far off, made them look to the stream. There, in the deepest part of the water, they saw a shimmering white reflection.

They both watched the ripples circling around a large rock.

"It's the man in the moon." Mark laughed. "He's fallen into the water."

"It's a beautiful lady," Alice said. "She's waiting
in the water for a—"

"A frog!" yelled Mark. "Look on the rock. It's a
frog—an ugly frog."

"Beautiful," Alice murmured.

"Ugly," Mark answered.

"Beautiful," Alice said.

"Ugly. Ugly."

"Beautiful."

The sound of their voices rose higher, and they turned around to face each other. They were glaring now, their faces angry, and they drew close together, their arms outflung, ready to fight. Alice reached out to grab Mark, and as she did so the flower fell from his hat and into the stream. Mark leaned forward and pulled the flower from Alice's hat and threw it up on the wall.

Both looked at the flower floating away in the
water. The stream caught it and carried it out to
where the frog sat on the rock. Its bulging eyes,
rimmed in yellow, blinked at them for a moment.
Then, quickly, it jumped into the water. In the ripples the petals of the flower disappeared.

Alice turned back slowly to where her flower lay on the wall. There beside it she saw in the dusk, the sticky white trail that drew her eyes to a large, black creature.

"Look, Mark," she said, reaching out for his hand. "Look, it's a snail."

"Snail?" Mark questioned.

"Of course, you silly," she answered, climbing up on the wall and crouching down on her knees. "It's a snail."

Mark walked back to the wall. Somehow he ought to have known. Somehow, he thought, looking into the trees, he might have known it. If only Alice had turned around and helped him before.

Alice was talking to the snail now, telling her to go hide under a leaf, for night was almost here. Mark

stood waiting. His feet were cold, and his coat wasn't warm enough. His flower was gone, and he gazed out to the rock where the frog had appeared, where the water had taken his flower. Then, just at the spot where they had been, a shadow fluttered in the pool from overhead, and down swooped a beautiful bird. It settled on the rock.

"Look," he whispered to Alice. "It's come down."

"What?" she asked.

"Your friend in the sky," he told her. "Your bird."

"Bird?"

"Of course, silly," he said. "You were calling to it and it came."

"You should have told me he was a bird," Alice said, coming down from the wall to the stream bed.

"You should have told me she was a snail."

They stood there now, moving from one foot to another, for the rocks and the ground were cold. They huddled together for warmth, and the trees began to move a bit in the wind.

From somewhere near the path a voice called their names.

"Shall we listen?" Mark asked.

The rocks had lost their color now. The sun was gone. They turned back to the wall to say good night to the snail, but it had left. The bird was no longer on the rock. The water was turning bright in the moon's reflection.

Mark reached out and took the flower from the wall and put it back into Alice's hat.

"It's time to go," Alice said.

"Yes," Mark answered.